Dinkle Smiff's Moggies

Tibby

Story by Eve White
Illustrations by Deborah Yoder

This book is a work of fiction. Places, events, and situations in this story are purely fictional and any resemblance to actual persons, living or dead, is coincidental.

© 2004 Eve White
All Rights Reserved.

No part of this book may be reproduced, stored in a retrieval system, or transmitted by any means without the written permission of the author.

First published by AuthorHouse 11/01/04

ISBN: 1-4208-0199-6 (sc)

Library of Congress Control Number: 2004097959

Printed in the United States of America
Bloomington, Indiana

This book is printed on acid-free paper.

1663 LIBERTY DRIVE
BLOOMINGTON, INDIANA 47403
(800) 839-8640
www.authorhouse.com

DINKLE SMIFF's MOGGIES

Thank You

Many thanks to Deb Yoder, an exceptionally gifted artist with a great passion for detail and color. It was a pleasure working with her and experiencing her enthusiasm while making my book come to life. Without her help I think I would have decided once again to put my books in mothballs for another day.

Thank you, Deb, from the bottom of my heart.   Let's do it again!

Love, Eve

My thanks go to Emily Hacker who modeled for Dink. The resemblance is amazing once the spectacles are put in place. Thank you, Emily. You are precious.

Love, Mrs. White

Thanks also go to my husband, Ken, who, I am happy to say, is a great cook. He kept me sustained while I was slogging away at the typewriter!   If I were the cook in the family (heaven forbid) we would have withered away from malnutrition, and people would be reading our obituaries rather than Dinkle Smiff's Moggies.

Love, Eve

Tibby

DINKLE SMIFF's MOGGIES

Tibby

My name is Tibby. I am Dinkle Smiff's first "moggie", otherwise known as a cat. Dinkle was born in London, England, before the second world war, and so was I. Dinkle was a very sweet, kind little girl with blonde hair and spectacles, and I first saw her when I was a tiny kitten. Her father found me one day on his way home from work.

The first thing I remember was a bitterly cold day, and I was sitting all by myself under the bushes by the side of the road. I was cold and wet and hungry. I didn't know where the rest of my family was, and I was lost! Suddenly, a hand came down and scooped me up and put me into a deep pocket. I was not very happy about being put into a pocket, and I wriggled around and tried my hardest to escape. I was very angry at whoever had picked me up; I was not used to human beings. As a matter of fact, this was the first human being I had ever been near. I realized later that it was Mr. Smiff who had picked me up.

I heard the strangest noises while I was in that pocket – apparently I was on a tram because I could feel the motion and could hear the clickety-clack of the wheels, and there were people everywhere; I was not used to people. I started to shudder because I was VERY scared, and every now and then when I could not stop shaking with fright, this gentle hand would stroke my head and scratch me under my chin very tenderly. Mr. Smiff would speak to me in a very soft voice, telling me not to be scared, and that I would like it where I was going.

When the tram stopped, Mr. Smiff got off, and I went with him, still in his pocket. He walked slowly down the road, talking to me all the time. We went a LONG way and then we stopped and I heard a key go into a lock. Mr. Smiff opened the door, closed it, and then walked up the 14 steps that would take us into the kitchen. I heard him say "Where's Dinkle? Tell her I've got something for her." At that moment the gentle hand reached in and took me out very carefully. Oh, goodness gracious me – the lights were so bright – I blinked a few times, and then, there she was – Dinkle Smiff. She stood in front of me wearing a red blouse , a gray pleated skirt, gray woolen socks which came up to her knees, and a pair of indoor house slippers with bows on them. She looked at me and I looked at her, and it was love at first sight! "Oh, Dad, where did you find her? She is a lovely color, and she is <u>SO TINY!</u>" Mr. Smiff told Dinkle he had found me waiting to be picked up and given a home. He said he thought I was a feral cat, which is a wild cat, and that I might not fit in with the family and might have to be let outside to take care of myself when I got bigger.

Anyway, Dinkle Smiff gave her Dad a big kiss, picked me up and took me over to her mother who was in the middle of preparing dinner. OOOHHH, dinner!!! Dinner was FOOD – I had not had any food for days! Before anyone knew what was going on, I had jumped out of Dink's arms and onto the dinner table. There were screams of disapproval from Mr. and Mrs. Smiff and Dink. I was grabbed by the scruff of the neck by Mr. Smiff and he said "All right young fella m' lad, the first thing we have to teach you is some table manners! You just must NOT get on the table, no matter how good the food smells, and no matter how hungry you are!" All my short gray hairs stood on end and I SPAT at Mr. Smiff - I hissed and I growled! I was SO angry. "Ah ha, young fella m' lad, we have a temper, do we?" said Mr. Smiff. "Let's talk about this." (Mr. Smiff always called me "young fella, m' lad" even though I am a **LITTLE GIRL** – **NOT A BOY**!)

I looked around and there was Dink with tears in her eyes, Mrs. Smiff was standing by the table pouring a cup of tea, and Mr. Smiff still had me by the scruff of my neck, and they were ALL looking at ME! Well, I was not a very polite kitten, and I continued to SPIT. How dare these people take me in where I did not want to go, and how dare they say they wanted to talk to me!

Mr. Smiff sat me on his lap and gently let go of my neck, but he held me firmly because he knew I would scamper away. While he held me, Mrs. Smiff poured some delicious brown gravy into a saucer and she left it on the table until it cooled down; she added some mashed potatoes and just a few pieces of meat. Dink was stroking me gently all the time and telling me that everything was all right, then Mrs. Smiff brought over the bowl of food and put it on the floor. Mr. Smiff lowered me to the ground, stroked my head, and told me to fill my boots! I don't think he meant that – he meant for me to fill my tummy, but I was soon to find out that Mr. Smiff said all kinds of funny things which made Dink giggle.

After dinner, the whole family sat down by the fireside and decided what my name should be. Mr. Smiff suggested all kinds of funny names, but they settled on TIBBY.

That night I was taken to bed with Dink and I slept all night long. I had never been so warm and cozy – EVER. When I woke up in the morning and jumped off the bed, I followed my nose to the smell of food in the kitchen. There was a saucer of warm milk on the kitchen floor for me – it was scrumptious! I guess I had a kind of frown on my face because I was not sure of bathroom manners, and Mr. Smiff took me over to a corner of the scullery where there was newspaper on the floor and a tray of ashes on top of it. I curled up in the ashes to take a nap, and Mr. Smiff said "No, silly – you don't sleep in it – you use the bathroom in it!" Goodness gracious me, I must say I did feel silly, but I never forgot what that tray of ashes was for after that.

Life was absolutely lovely with the Smiffs. Every morning Mrs. Smiff prepared breakfast for Mr. Smiff before he went off to work. Dink slept late because she was not old enough to go to school at that time, so Mrs. Smiff would always take time out to sit by the fire with me on her lap, and I would stay there while she drank a cup of tea. On that first morning when Dink got out of bed and after she had had her breakfast, she took me next door to meet Grannie Litchfield. Grannie was a very tiny lady with silvery gray hair, and when she saw me she threw her hands up in the air and exclaimed "What a beautiful kitten, and such a lovely color," and she proceeded to tell Dink that I was a short-haired gray, almost smoky blue, maybe even a Russian blue! I was beginning to feel VERY IMPORTANT - I was a short-haired gray, almost smoky blue! I didn't know that. And being a Russian blue sounded EXTREMELY IMPORTANT! I guess there were a lot of things I didn't know!

A few days later Dink and Mrs. Smiff carried me to the veterinarian, the dreaded cat doctor, to get me "looked at" to see if I was healthy. When we went through the door there was a loud ringing bell that let them know someone was coming in, which scared me half out of my wits to start with, and then there was that gosh awful parrot that screeched "Hullo – hullo" and proceeded to sing "happy birthday to you, happy birthday to you" at the top of its lungs. I tell you, this was no way to treat a Russian blue!! But when I met Dr. Alley and Dr. King and their staff of sweet ladies who kept telling me I was so "booooful", I relaxed, got examined, was given a clean bill of health, and I never minded going there again, except for that parrot!!

One thing I remember very well. When Dink was small she had to be taken to the hospital. I was scared when two men came upstairs with a stretcher to take Dink away. I didn't like that one bit, and sat on the banister rail and hissed and growled and wouldn't let the men come past me, as I did not want Dink to be taken away. Grannie Litchfield picked me up gently and took me into the kitchen and shut the door and told me that Dink would not be gone for very long, that the doctors and nurses at the hospital would make her well, and she would come right back to us. I missed Dink SO MUCH, and it seemed ages before she came home. I would sit looking out of the upstairs window hoping that the ambulance would bring her back, and then one day, there it was. I saw Dink get out and she looked straight up at the window and waved to me. I was out of the front room and down the stairs before anyone could say "Jack Robinson" and the next thing I knew, Dink had scooped me up, kissed me, and carried me back upstairs where Mrs. Smiff and Grannie had tea waiting for us. They had salmon and cucumber sandwiches, crumpets and scones and clotted cream, and guess what I liked the best? First, the salmon, and then the <u>C-R-E-A-M</u> !!   Well, Dink was home and things were back to normal again. I asked Dink if her doctor had a singing parrot like my doctor did, but he didn't. Of course, who did I sleep with that night? -- DINKLE SMIFF!!

We had a lovely time together, the whole family, and we were very close. It was just one lazy day after another; all the days were practically the same. I used to help Mrs. Smiff with the housework – well, I did what I could. Whichever room we were in, when Mrs. Smiff mopped under the couch or back of the china cabinet, I would be right there to see if she had found any of my toys, and when she did, I would pounce on them and go scampering down the hall with them. Sometimes I would knock them through the banister rails and they would bounce down the stairs and come to rest on the rug in the hallway. Most times they would stay there until Mr. Smiff came home from work, and he would say "Hullo, who's been cleaning house today? Are these toys ready for the dust bin?" and Dink would scream "No, they belong to Tibby" and Mr. Smiff would put them in an old shoe box where all my toys were kept. I had several little woolen balls which Dink had made for me. She used to get a milk bottle top which had a hole in the middle, and she would push the wool through, around and around, until it was full, then Mrs. Smiff would cut the edges and tie a piece of wool around the middle and leave a long piece of wool for Dink to hold, and she would run through the house pulling the ball of wool behind her, with me in hot pursuit trying to catch it. I always did, and somehow I always lost it, but it would always turn up on cleaning day somewhere in the house.

I found out what a special time of year Christmas was. Dink and her friends would make paper chains to stretch across the ceiling in the living room. They cut colored paper into strips and put paste on the ends to stick it together to make them into circles, and then would fasten all the circles together to make them into chains. Of course, I helped with that job by batting any loose circles around the room, only to be yelled at by one of the girls, and the circle snatched away to be added to the chain. I did my best to help, but

I got my feet stuck in the paste and was eventually banished to another room so the girls could finish the job and get the chains hung around the ceiling. Grannie and Mrs. Smiff always made a delicious Christmas pudding ahead of time, to be served with hot custard, which everyone enjoyed after Christmas dinner. They also made a wonderful fruit cake encased in marzipan with a hard white icing on the top and around the sides; this would be served with sandwiches and Ovaltine at tea time.

There was always a Christmas Eve party when the whole family got together to decorate the tree. Most of the ornaments were hand-made. Aunts and uncles and cousins would drop by to help and they would sit around laughing and talking about old times, and how this year they had all done their shopping at Clapham Junction on a very foggy day when they could hardly see a hand in front of them. The fog was so bad that the conductor had to walk on the pavement just in front of the tram with a flashlight so that the driver could see where he had to stop to pick up passengers, and when it got to be a real pea-souper, they all got off the tram and walked home with their own flashlights trying to feel their way through the fog. They must have all found their way home because no one was missing at the house on Christmas Eve. Came time for everyone to go home, and Dink and I went to bed early because Father Christmas would be coming down the chimney with presents for us all.

On Christmas morning we all got up early. When Dink and I got to the living room there were all kinds of little packages under the tree which had not been there when we went to bed, so Father Christmas had come in the night, and everyone agreed that they had not heard him arrive, but the plate and tea cup which had been left on the hearth were empty . Mr. and Mrs. Smiff and Grannie were already there, smiling brightly and sipping their tea, just waiting for Dink and me to come in. This was the time for presents to be handed out. Mrs. Smiff got a box of embroidered handkerchiefs and a box of chocolates. Mr. Smiff got a new shaving brush and mug. There was a lovely flowered pinafore for Grannie. Dink got a pair of warm red slippers, some woolen gloves and a hat, and there was a crocheted (pronounced CROSHAYED) ball with a string attached to it for me. The family all went off to church and came back with cold fingers and red noses. What a lovely Christmas it was. We were all healthy and happy, and as soon as everyone was warmed up, we sat down to our lovely dinner. What more could anyone ask?

By now it was time for Dink to start school. She looked so smart in her school uniform with the white blouse and navy blue gym slip. She loved school and was very soon an avid book worm. Books, books and more books, but she still had a lot of time left for me. Sometimes she would even read to me, and I loved it. Most times while she read I would sit on her lap, and her hand was always close by to chuck me under the chin or rub my ears. I used to while away my time while Dink was at school. Sometimes I would go next door with Grannie and Aunt Mill. They were always so kind to me. I spent a lot of my time looking out the window. There was always something going on. Aunt Kate lived across the street, and every afternoon a dog would turn up on her door step around about 3:00 o'clock. Aunt Kate would open the door and bring out a saucer of warm tea which the dog would drink, and off he would go and I would not see him again until the next afternoon. Sometimes he turned up early, and Aunt Kate would say "No, it isn't teatime yet; go home and come back later." And he would – and on his second trip he would bark loudly to be sure that Aunt Kate had not forgotten his afternoon tea break. I watched as the children went to school, then around about 10:00 o'clock the ladies would be outside sweeping or scrubbing their doorsteps. After they had done that, off they would trot with their grocery baskets to go "up the road shopping." This was a daily ritual for all mums. There were no refrigerators in those days. The meat, fish and vegetables were fresh from the shops every day. The children would come home from school at lunch time, and after lunch there was always a scurry of feet heading back to school as most children left it until the last minute to go out the door.

From the window I saw all sorts of people. There was the postman with his bag of letters; he came three times a day. The rag and bone man walked down the street with his wheelbarrow collecting old clothes or furniture that nobody wanted anymore. The knife sharpening man came on his bicycle and the neighbors would take their dinner knives out to be sharpened. The coal man came once every two weeks and he would carry a huge sack of coal up our stairs and deposit it in the coal bin at the top of the stairs. I always thought that must be such a hard job carrying all that coal every day. The gas meter man came once a month and Mrs. Smiff would open the cupboard under the dish cabinet so that he could shine his flashlight in there to read how much gas we had used for the month, then we would pay him what we owed. Speaking of gas, I was always most intrigued with the man who came down the street every night as it was getting dark. He carried a long cane with a flame on the top of it, and he would jiggle the lamp to turn the gas street lights on, and then in the mornings he would come back again to turn them all off. We lived close to the railway yards and when the railway man would drive his horse and cart down the street delivering packages to and from the trains, there were always a bunch of boys who would be hanging on the back of the cart having a free ride down the street. Oh, and the chimney sweep – he was called mostly in the autumn to clean the chimneys before the fires had to be lit for winter. I always had to giggle when the sweep's brush popped out of the top of the chimneys across the street. I just loved that!

One day Dink went to school in the morning as usual, then came home early. Mrs. Smiff packed all Dink's clothes and hair brush and tooth brush into a pillow case. I wondered what was going on. Mrs. Smiff wrote Dink's name and address on a label and pinned it onto her coat. Dink started to cry. She picked me up and kissed me and hugged me tight. Her tears ran down her cheeks onto mine, and she was gone! I sat by the fire and licked my paws and washed my face with Dink's tears. What could have happened? Later that day Mrs. Smiff came back home without Dink. Mr. Smiff came home from work and Grannie came over from next door. Soon Aunt Mill and Aunt Kate dropped by. Tea was served and the events of the day unfolded. I learned that the war had started and that bombs would be dropping on London, and the government had decided it would be best if the children were sent to the countryside where they would be safe. There were bus loads of children being dropped off at the railway station with their teachers and parents. Mrs. Smiff kissed Dink goodbye as she left her at the station with her teacher, Miss Eader,. They were headed for Reading in Berkshire, and Miss Eader promised all the mothers that she would have their children write home as soon as they could. Back home in the kitchen, everyone was talking about how awful it was and how frightened the children must be. Mr. Smiff was also going to have to leave as he was needed to serve in the British Merchant Navy. I just could not believe all this commotion had happened, upsetting everyone and changing our lives for ever. I was sitting on Grannie's lap and everybody held hands and said a silent prayer for everyone's safety.

When the postman put the letters through the letter box a few days later, Mrs. Smiff ran downstairs to pick them up off the mat. There was a letter from Dink. Grannie Litchfield came over, followed by Aunt Mill and Aunt Kate, and Mrs. Smiff read Dink's letter out loud. It read:

"Dear Mum and Dad,

We are in Reading. Jeannie Singfield and I became friends on the train. When we got to Reading there were all kinds of ladies waiting there; small ones, tall ones, thin ones, chubby ones, and they all picked out the children they wanted to take home. All the ladies and children were soon gone, and just Jeannie and I were left with our teacher, Miss Eader, with nowhere to go. Then a lady named Mrs. Harris arrived and said she would take one of us. Miss Eader asked if she would please take the both of us for the night as it was so late, and we could work it out the next morning. Jeannie and I both went home with a very bad-tempered Mrs. Harris who put us up in her attic where we slept on an old mattress on the floor. We both cried ourselves to sleep. We are still with Mrs. Harris and she really doesn't want us. We wondered why she even turned up at the station, until we heard today that the government will pay her for each child she takes care of.

We will start to school tomorrow and we heard that Miss Eader will be our teacher. She is a very nice lady and has brought her mother with her. They are staying at the vicarage.

I will write again next week. Please write to me as soon as you can. Give my love to everyone, and tell TIBBY I miss her. Mrs. Harris does not have any pets.

Love from Dink.   X X X

X X

X "

It was not long before Mrs. Smiff and Mrs. Singfield went down to Reading and brought the girls home. Oh, what a lovely day that was for everyone. It was wonderful having Dink back again. She did not stay long but while she was back home she and her school chums knitted scarves, socks, gloves and Balaclava hats for the solders, sailors and air force men. While Dink did her knitting, if the ball of wool fell off her lap onto the floor, I would pounce on it and bat it all around the living room. Dink would scream and say "No, Tibby, that's not a toy, it's for the sailors." And she would run across the room and pick up the ball of wool, give me a loving scratch under my chin, and go back to her knitting. The three different services had different colors for their uniforms – navy blue for the Navy, gray for the Air Force, and khaki for the Army. Dink knitted all her things in navy blue, as Mr. Smiff went into the British Navy; actually, he went into the British Merchant Navy. His ships brought food from other countries back to England during the war. He went to India, Africa, and even went as far as the United States of America one time and brought Dink back a doll from the World's Fair in New York. She was very proud of that doll, and I was not allowed to touch it.

As the war went on and the bombs began to drop on the houses, Dink was sent away to the country to live with her aunt and uncle in Tipton-St. John's in Devonshire. She loved it there, but we both missed each other very much. I was left in London with Mrs. Smiff and Grannie Litchfield, and they would talk to me and let me sleep on their laps while they enjoyed a cup of tea together each afternoon, and they always included me with my bowl of warm milk. It was a nice quite time for a while, but I did miss Dink and Mr. Smiff, and I would listen to Mrs. Smiff and Grannie talk about them and read their letters while they enjoyed their cups of tea. Mind you, it was not always nice and quiet. When the bombs dropped, it was very scary and I used to run and hide under the couch just shaking if I was in the house by myself. At night-time I used to sleep in bed with Mrs. Smiff, right down under the covers with her. She was kind to let me do that, but I really think she enjoyed my company as much as I enjoyed hers.

One night the bombing was so bad that Mrs. Smiff and Grannie and Aunt Kate and Aunt Mill from next door all went to the shelter but they couldn't take me with them. Mrs. Smiff gave me a kiss and told me I'd be all right and they would be back in the morning. Well – I was not all right! All of a sudden this great bomb fell nearby and blew the windows out and blew the front door off. I was so terrified, I really don't know what I did. I guess I just panicked because I jumped out of the shattered front window and kept running and running in the dark, not knowing where I was going, but just wanting to get away from the bombs. This was the first time I had been outside the house since Mr. Smiff had picked me up all that time ago. Eventually, I stopped running and hid under a shed in someone's garden. When daylight came I ventured out and looked around. I didn't recognize anything. I was **LOST!** I was scared for the first time since Mr. Smiff took me home when I was a kitten. I walked and walked, and I ran and hid under something when anyone approached me. I did not like to talk to strangers and I didn't want them touching me. I just longed for Dinkle Smiff to come and snatch me up and take me home, but it didn't happen. I was hungry and I was cold. There was no warm milk and no nice fire to sit by. I cried myself to sleep so many times. Days and nights went by and I was hungry. I had to learn to catch mice, and I did a pretty good job of it. I had to drink rain water from the pavement, and I was lucky that it did rain quite often. Children would find me sometimes and try to catch me. I suppose they were trying to be nice, but I kept running away from them. I stayed by myself all the time. Sometimes at night there were other cats in the neighborhood but we never got along. I never made friends with another cat. There were lots of nights when bombs dropped and I never got used to it – I was scared all the time – and most nights I would dream of Dink and Mr. and Mrs. Smiff, and wish things were as safe as they used to be, with us all together in the kitchen having dinner and then off to a nice warm bed – ooooh - I would think all the time how nice it would be to be sitting by the fireside again. Would those days ever come back, or would I always be walking through the streets, scared and hungry? During the daytime when I felt safe coming out, I would watch people go by and hope that it was one of the Smiffs, but no matter how hard I tried, I never could find them or my house. I met a dog one day and wondered what on earth it was – it chased me and I ran underneath something where he could not reach me. He barked and barked and made an awful racket, he ran around and around, peering under the place where I was flat against the wall, hoping he could not get under. He never did; he eventually went away, and I was glad! I stayed under there and fell asleep, not coming out until daylight the next day.

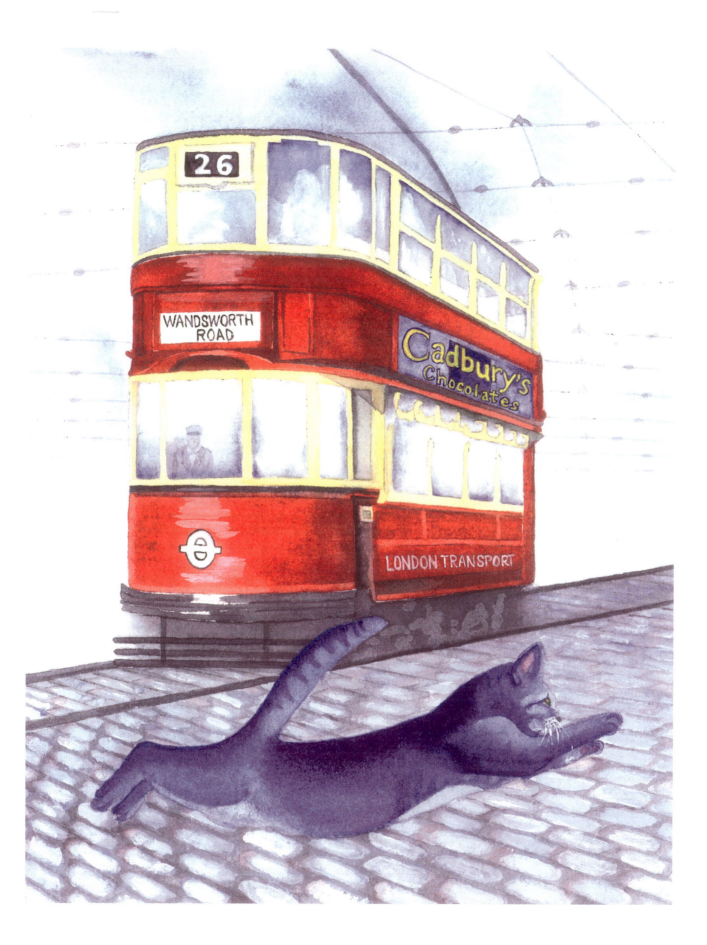

One day I ventured up the hill and there was a busy main road and I started to run across when this great "thing" came at me. A bell started to clang and I heard someone say "Oh, no!" but I kept running, and the "thing" missed me, and I heard someone say "That cat nearly got run over by a tram." I was shaking so badly and went to hide, as usual. I was so sick and tired of hiding. I was lying in my hiding place and thinking about what had happened when I suddenly remembered that it was a tram that Mr. Smiff first took me home on. I guess this was the first time I had heard a tram and its clanging bell since that time long ago. I began to think about that and wondered, being as the tram was here, could the Smiffs' house be very far away? My heart began to beat fast and I decided right there and then that if I was to find my way home I just had to forget about being scared and get out there and look around. So, that very minute I marched back across the road, with no trams in sight this time, and went back down the hill. I tried to remember which way Mr. Smiff had walked that night when I was a tiny kitten, but it was no use; I had been too young and was in a pocket, so it was really useless. Nevertheless, I kept walking. There were some air raid shelters along one side of the road and I was able to get into one of them to spend the night and catch some mice for supper. Every day I would go out and look around up and down the streets and go back to the air raid shelter at night. No one was in the shelters because apparently no bombs had dropped for a long time now.

One day it was different outside. People were all out of their houses, talking and singing and dancing. There were tables being put up in the streets and someone had dragged a piano out onto the pavement, and someone had put up a drum set, someone else had an accordion, someone else had a trumpet. There were sandwiches and cakes put on the tables, lemonade was being served, all the neighbors were outside, the band was playing old songs, and people were singing and dancing – even the children were singing and dancing, and they knew the words to all the songs. Everybody was wearing funny paper party hats. I had never seen anything like that in my life, except when we used to wear our funny paper hats at Christmastime.

I was watching all this going on and started to walk down the street when all of a sudden I heard someone scream "TIBBY, is that you?" I looked up at the lady and it was Mrs. Smiff. She came over to me very gently to be sure it was me, she stroked me and made sure, then she picked me up in her arms and carried me back to the house. The windows had been repaired and the front door had been put back on its hinges. She put some milk on the hob to warm and broke up some bread and put it in the milk. When the milk was warm enough, Mrs. Smiff put it on the floor for me. It was **SO GOOD!** Even the bread tasted good. After I had emptied the bowl, I sat there and washed my face and paws for the first time in months.

In the meantime, Mrs. Smiff had called Grannie to come over from next door. They put the kettle on and made a pot of tea, and here we were sitting by the fire like old times, with me on one lap or the other, depending on which one picked me up. They did make such a fuss of me, and I found myself purring, which I know I had not done since that night when the bomb had dropped. I heard Grannie say "Listen to that purr – it gets louder by the minute. How long did you say Tibby has been gone?" "Well," said Mrs. Smiff, "it has been about six months. I wonder where she has been? I thought I never would see her again. What do you think Dink will say when she gets home?" Oh, goodness me, I was so happy to be here that I really hadn't thought about Dink. How could I not think about my best friend?

Mrs. Smiff and Grannie left me in the house sitting by the warm fire while they went out to join the street party. Before they went, Mrs. Smiff hugged me close and said "Tibby, **THE WAR IS OVER.** No more bombs, no more noise. Mr. Smiff will soon be home from the sea, and we can all be a family again." And, off they went to the party.

Street Party

I guess I slept through it all, because it was almost dark when I heard Mrs. Smiff and Dink coming up the stairs. Before they came into the kitchen I heard Mrs. Smiff say, "Dink, if you could make a wish right now, what would it be?" There was silence for a minute while Dink thought about it, and she said "I would wish for Dad to be home, safe and sound." I think a frown came across my face as she said that, but it didn't last long, for Mrs. Smiff then said "And who else would you like to see back home?" Dink immediately said "Well, I would love to have Tibby back, but I guess she's gone for ever. I do miss her. Mum, do you think she is safe? Where do you suppose she might be?" Mrs. Smiff said "Well, if you go into the kitchen very quietly and don't frighten her, you might just find someone you know." On went the light and there was Dink just staring at me. She rushed across the room, picked me up and put me across her shoulder, cuddled me tight, sat down, kissed me and kissed me until I thought I would faint, and then just cried and cried! I don't know who was the happiest, Dink or me! She asked me where I had been all this time, and told me how everyone had been looking for me. Then she asked if I had anything to eat? A whole flock of questions she aimed at me, and I wish I could have answered her. All we both knew was that we were so happy to be back together again. Dink said, "Mum, we must write a letter to Dad to let him know that Tibby is back and that we can't wait for him to come back, too."

We all went to the front room window and looked outside at the party still going on. Someone had saved some Chinese lanterns from before the war and they were on the table to light up the festivities. People were having such a grand time. There was a knock at the front door and Mrs. Smiff went down to answer it. The next thing we knew, Mr. Smiff was there in the room behind us, arms outstretched, with a big smile on his face. He looked the same as I remembered him. Dink rushed over to give him a hug and kiss, and she said "I was just going to write you a letter. Look who came home." Dink put me in Mr. Smiff's arms, and his hands were as gentle as always when he rubbed me under my chin. "Well, young fella m' lad," he said, "you tell me where you've been all this time, and I'll tell you where I've been!" He still called me "young fella m' lad" but that was all right. Mr. and Mrs. Smiff and Dink all laughed and we went to the kitchen for dinner. It was just like the first night I got there, except that this time I remembered not to jump on the table, but I did get my gravy and mashed potatoes in my dish on the floor while they all ate at the table.

We were all back home – Mr. Smiff back from the sea, Dink back from the countryside, and me back from who knows where? And Mr. Smiff was there ready to take care of us all again. We were **HOME!** I slept with Dink in her bed that night, warm as toast, and we fell asleep listening to the music and singing outside in the street. I wondered if Dink could hear the music above the noise of my purring!!

GOOD NIGHT, GOD BLESS!

About the Author

Eve Smith White grew up in London during World War II. Her stories are based on true life events from her childhood. As the British like to give nicknames to each other, Eve's father nicknamed her Dinkle (shortened to Dink). Smith, Eve's family name, was pronounced "Smiff', which is a true Cockney pronunciation. Moggie is a British name for cat; hence the name "Dinkle Smiff's Moggies." This is the first in a series of eight books chronicling the adventures of all the stray cats that have come into the Smiff household since Tibby, and Tibby has pronounced herself matriarch of all the subsequent orphans who have turned up on the doorstep, or within "close" proximity.

Eve now lives in Nashville, Tennessee with her husband, Ken, and several moggies. Their two sons live close by. Kent and his wife, Jenny, have three moggies. Steve and his daughter, Jessica, have two moggies and two rescued Labrador retrievers.

Eve's upcoming book will be about Scruffy and Snowy, "A Tale of Two Kitties".

CPSIA information can be obtained
at www.ICGtesting.com
Printed in the USA
LVIC06n0051150114
369441LV00003B/4